# Depression
# naturally treated with
# Homeopathy and Schuessler salts
# (homeopathic cell salts)

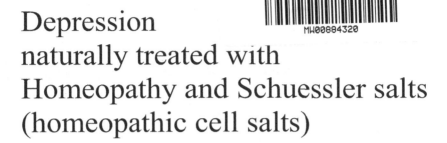

Robert Kopf

# CONTENT

# INTRODUCTION

Robert Kopf, Author of Naturopathy and Traditional healer Translated from german edition by the author.

Depression can happen at any age and is a serious mood disorder. It can result in behavioral and health problems that affect every area of life. It affects how you feel and think and can lead to a variety of emotional and physical problems.

Depression isn't a weakness, nor is it something that you can simply "snap out".

Symptoms caused by depression vary from person to person and include personality changes, feelings of sadness, emptiness, unhappiness, hopelessness, angry outbursts, panic disorder, irritability, loss of interest or pleasure in normal activities, sleep disturbances, tiredness, reduced appetite and weight loss or increased cravings for food and weight gain, anxiety, agitation, feelings of worthlessness, thoughts of death, suicidal thoughts, unexplained physical problems and chronic pains.

A variety of factors may cause depression such as changes in the body's balance of hormones (thyroid problems, menopause, pregnancy), an acidification of the body, inherited traits, stressful or traumatic events, abuse of alcohol or illegal drugs, chronic illness (cancer, diabetes, heart disease), social isolation, low self-esteem, loneliness, vitamin D deficiency, arteriosclerosis and metabolic disorders.

In the homeopathic and biochemical treatment (Schuessler salts) of depression, detoxification therapies serve the activation of metabolism, the immune system and strengthening the body's nerves, circulation and connective tissue.

It cleans, de-acidifies the body, is mineralizing and leads to a balanced life energy.

Depression can be caused and reinforced by a mineral deficiency and an acidification of the body. Mineral deficiency and acidification in turn weaken the hormonal system, nerves and immune system.

Also a defective metabolism favors depression, acidification and chronic health problems and is often the result of a disturbance of mineral intake and mineral distribution.

Although we may receive enough minerals in our food, in the event of a metabolic disorder, not all of the minerals may reach the cells.

The use of homeopathic remedies and Schuessler salts is a good way to compensate this mineral deficiency in a natural way and to treat depression.

First I like to explain you the therapies for the treatment and prevention of depression offered in this guide:

**Homeopathy** was developed about 200 years ago by Samuel Hahnemann. The three basic principles of Homeopathy are the simile rule, homeopathic drug testing and detection of individual disease.

The most important principle is the principle of Similarity (simile rule), which was formulated in 1796 by Hahnemann.

It states that a patient should be treated with the remedy, which can cause in its original state similar symptoms in healthy people like the existing disease. It notes primarily the main complaints of the patient.

Together with a few differentiating additional informations (modalities) then the right remedy will be found for the treatment of depression.

The dosage depends on the condition of the patient. As the patient improves, the distances between the medication will be gradually extended.

What happens if you choose the wrong remedy? Nothing - just as a key does not turn in the wrong door lock, a wrong homeopathic remedy does not cause any reaction in the body.

The homeopathic remedies are available as D-, C- and LM potencies.

For the beginners in Homeopathy, I recommend the use of lower D-potencies. Higher potencies (D200, C and LM potencies) should only be given by an expert, as they go very deep in their effects and are often used only once.

**Schuessler salts** (also named homeopathic cell salts, tissue salts, Biochemistry) for the treatment of depression

In the 19th century the german physician Dr. Wilhelm Heinrich Schuessler (1821 to 1898) developed his health cure with homeopathic mineral salts. In recent years this therapy celebrated a comeback.

In his studies Schuessler discovered twelve mineral compounds, comprised each of a base and an acid, which play a crucial role in the function and structure of the body. He developed his own system with which many diseases can be treated in a natural way.

Schuessler focused his search on mineral salts and trace elements, which are found in every cell of the body and called his method of healing "Biochemistry" (chemistry of life).

It is based on the assumption that nearly every disease is caused because of the lack of a specific mineral salt. This leads to dysregulations inside the cells. The molecules cannot flow freely.

A mineral salt deficiency arises from the fact that the cells cannot optimally use the minerals. To improve their absorption, mineral salts therefore have to be highly diluted (potentized).

Schuessler used the homeopathic potencies D3 (3x), D6 (6x) and D12 (12x) for his therapy. In general, the 6x (dilution 1:1 million) or 12x (1:1 trillion) is taken.

In this naturopathic adviser, I will give you recommendations how to treat and prevent depression naturally with Homeopathy, herbal tinctures and Schuessler salts.

I will present you the most proven homeopathic remedies and Schuessler salts, including the appropriate potency and dosage.

Naturopathy works holistically. It does not treat single symptoms only. It treats the whole body, mind and soul.

I wish you much success, joy in life and especially your health.

Robert Kopf

Robert Kopf

## Metabolic blockages in the treatment of depression

There are several metabolic blockages which you have to treat for to deacidify and detoxify the body of people suffering from depression.

Metabolic blockage No. 1: The acid-base balance

Too much sugar, white flour, meat and sausage acidifies the body. In order to neutralize the acids precious bases are consumed. What is not neutralized, ends up as a "hazardous waste" in the connective tissue and leads to its acidity.

The metabolic process slows down. We get depression, gain weight despite calorie conscious diet and exercise.

## Metabolic blockage No. 2: The connective tissue

The connective tissue is more than just a connection between the organs. It serves as a nutrient storage and intermediate storage of metabolic products.

In the connective tissue the cells dispose their waste products. That the toxins can leave the body, enough mineral salts must be present.

A mineral deficiency causes metabolic residues, acidification and overload with toxins. They remain in the connective tissue and bind water. It comes to depressive moods and water retention (edema) in the tissues of the body.

## Metabolic blockage No. 3: The digestion

Environmental pollution, lush diet and medication burden the liver, our central metabolic organ. Stomach, pancreas and intestines suffer with.

Many metabolic processes stalled and it comes to depressive moods, weight gain, constipation, bloating and stomach problems.

## Metabolic blockage No. 4: Our water Resources

Every day the organism produces acids and waste products that have to be filtered out by the kidneys. But part of it also ends up in the connective tissue, because for the removal mineral salts are absent. This forces depression.

## Metabolic blockage No. 5: The protein digestion

Protein is essential for the production of enzymes, hormones, muscles and the connective tissue. However, in the cleavage of proteins ammonia is formed (a strong cytotoxin). The liver converts the ammonia into non-toxic urea, which is excreted in the urine.

Therefore, a high intake of protein is a strong decontamination work for the liver and our two kidneys. This stimulates depression.

Metabolic blockage No. 6: The digestion of fat

We need fats because they provide essential fatty acids. Fat is also the best energy storage in times of need. The body hoards it especially in the thighs and hips, the abdomen and buttocks.

But the adipose tissue is also a deposit for toxins. This forces depressive moods.

Metabolic blockage No. 7: The carbohydrate digestion

Carbohydrates are energy pure. But in abundance they are also responsible for weight gain and acidification of the body. What is not burned, will be converted and stored in fat.

Especially sweets and white flour products are dangerous. They let the blood sugar level rise up rapidly. This leads to a strong insulin release.

Insulin normalizes blood sugar. At the same time burning fat is broken. Insulin leads fats from the meal in the fat stores of the body. In addition, it holds back water in the body and causes rapidly new hunger.

More information for the treatment of your metabolism you will find in my book:

Metabolism and Metabolic syndrome naturally treated with Homeopathy and Schuessler salts

## Depression - Treatment with Homeopathy

In addition to your homeopathic treatment of depression, you may make a de-acidification health cure of your body with the following recipe:

320 grams of Sodium bicarbonate
50 grams of Potassium hydrogen carbonate
70 grams of Calcium citrate (Calciumcitrat)
40 grams of Calcium phosphate (Calciumphosphat)
20 grams of Magnesium citrate (Magnesiumcitrat)

Dissolve 1 teaspoon daily at 10 o'clock in the morning (10 am) and at 4 o'clock in the afternoon (4 pm) in 250 ml of lukewarm water. Drink in small sips.

During the day time, in addition to your homeopathic treatment, drink 3 cups of tea for the kidneys. In the evening drink one cup of tea for the liver. This will clean the blood and connective tissue and the toxins, acids and metabolic waste products will be extracted quickly.

1) Liver support tea and detoxing the body:

Semen Cardui marianae 50.0 (milk thistle), Rhizoma Tormentillae 15.0 (bloodroot), Radix cum Herba Taraxaci 30.0 (dandelion root and herb), Fructi anisidine (anise) 20.0, Fructi Foeniculi (fennel) 20.0, Folia crispae mentha (mint) 15.0
Mix the above listed items together. Add 1 tablespoon into 1 cup (250 ml) cold water and cover for 8 hours. Cook 3 minutes. Let sit covered for 10 minutes and then strain. Drink 1 cup in the evening.

2) Tea for the kidneys and the extraction of metabolic waste and acids through the urinary tract:

Folia Betulae (birch leaves) 30.0, Herba urticae (nettle herb) 30.0, Herba Equiseti (horsetail) 20.0, Herba Virgaureae (goldenrod) 20.0
Mix the above listed ingredients together. Add 2 teaspoons into 1 cup (250 ml) of hot water, let sit covered for 10 minutes. Strain to drink. Drink 3 cups daily.

3) If you suffer from allergies, alternate daily the 2 above mentioned teas with a tea for the treatment of allergies to sensitize your body for the treatment of depression with Schuessler salts and Homeopathy:

Radix Imperatoriae 20 g, Radix Pimpinellae 20 g, Herba Euphrasiae 10 g, Herba Rutae hortensis 30 g, Rhizoma Graminis 10 g, Herba Absinthii 10 g
Mix the above listed ingredients together. Add 1 teaspoon into 1 cup (250 ml) of water, cook 2 minutes, let sit covered for 10 minutes. Strain to drink. Drink 3 cups daily.

Pay attention to an adequate hydration (water, tea, unsweetened juices).
The kidneys can extract metabolic waste products only if there is enough liquid available. If you exercise a lot, you need more fluid. The water supports the elimination of toxins and waste products in the metabolism. In addition, it prevents hunger.

Drink the most until the afternoon. In the evening drink as little as possible to relieve the bladder.

For enhancing the effect of the homeopathic medicine dissolve the globules in a small glas of water and drink in small sips. Swallow after 1 minute. For stirring please do not use metal spoon.

Do not count the globules in the hand. The manual welding destroys the sprayed drug.

Avoid during the homeopathic treatment the consumption of nicotine, alcohol and spicy foods. They reduce the effectiveness of the sensitive homeopathic remedies.

**Abrotanum 3x**

Depression due to circulatory disorders in the brain.
Abrotanum opens the small arteries and veins (capillaries).
As a result, the blood flow is stimulated.
Increases blood circulation in the brain.
Sharp urine
Kidney and bladder diseases.
Stimulates the metabolism and the immune system.
3 times a day, take 10 globules, let them melt in your
mouth.

**Absinthium tincture**

Depression due to metabolic disorders.
The basic remedy for the treatment of metabolic disorders
due to stomach and liver weakness.
Strengthen the immune system, extracts environmental
toxins and resolves metabolic blockages.
Gastritis and stomach diseases.
Stimulates the function of the pancreas.
Promotes the formation of bile - the intestine is stimulated
by it (70% of our immune system are located in the
intestines). Intestines healthy, man healthy!
Bloating
3 times a day, add 15 drops in some water and drink in
small sips.

**Acidum iodatum 12x** (Acidum jodatum D12)
Depression due to calcification and hardening of the blood vessels.
2 times a day, take 5 globules, let them melt in your mouth.

**Acidum muriaticum 4x**
Depression
Arteriosclerosis and atherosclerosis
Acidum muriaticum enhances the absorption of iron in the small intestine (important for the treatment of depression).
3 times a day, take 10 globules, let them melt in your mouth.

## Acidum nitricum 6x

Depression

Strengthens the nerves of people suffering from depression, because stress weakens the immune system.

Acidum nitricum strengthens the immune system and the energy.

Heart problems and insomnia.

The person has a cold quickly.

Malodorous secretions

Strong smelling urine.

The face is dark and looks dried out.

The patient asks for salty and fatty foods.

A very nervous person. Life weariness, hopelessness, rejects consolation.

The patient has a "band feeling" around the head.

3 times a day, take 5 globules, let them melt in your mouth.

**Acidum phosphoricum 6x**

An important metabolic remedy for the treatment of depression.

Normalizes the metabolism and resolves metabolic blockages.

Acidum phosphoricum strengthen the nerves and immune system.

The patient is tired and weak.

Loss of concentration, dizziness.

Needs rest and warmth.

3 times a day, take 5 globules, let them melt in your mouth.

**Acidum sulph 6x** (Acidum sulfuricum D6)

Depression of women in menopause.

Nervousness and anxiety

Heart problems and sleep disorders.

Worse at night, in movement and touch.

Vomiting, nausea and sweating.

3 times a day, take 5 globules, let them melt in your mouth

## Aconitum napellua 6x

Akute depression, nervousness and neurasthenia.

Sensitive to weather changes.

Agony and delusions

The person is anxious, nervous, restless, hasty and frightened.

Retching and vomiting with fear and sweat.

Touch sensitiveness of the belly.

The main symptoms:

Dry and cold winds generate and aggravate the symptoms.

Restlessness

Worse in warm room, at night, by dry and cold winds.

Feverish restlessness

The accompanying symptoms:

Tingling, numbness, redness, heat.

People with dark hair and dark eyes.

3 times a day, take 5 globules, let them melt in your mouth.

**Adonis vernalis tincture**
Depression due to cardiac insufficiency and low blood pressure.
Adonis vernalis invigorates the heart.
3 times a day, add 15 drops in a small glass of water. Drink in small sips.

**Agaricus muscarius 6x**
Depression
A feeling as if frozen.
Feeling of stiffness
Involuntary twitching of muscles.
Sleeplessness
Nervousness and hot flashes.
3 times a day, take 5 globules, let them melt in your mouth.

**Agnus castus 3x**

Depression of women in menopause.

Menopausal symptoms

Weather sensitivity and mood swings.

Agnus castus has a regulating effect on the female hormonal system.

3 times a day, take 10 globules, let them melt in your mouth.

**Agrimonia eupatoria 3x**

Depression

Acidification and overload of the body with toxins due to a weakness of the digestive organs.

Stimulates digestion, metabolism and the immune system.

Strengthens the stomach, liver, pancreas and intestines (more then 70% of our immune system are located in the intestines).

Edema due to a liver weakness.

Bloating

Agrimonia promotes the formation of urea and the extraction of toxins.

Helps to strengthen the defense.

Purifies and detoxifies the body.

3 times a day, take 10 globules, let them melt in your mouth.

**Allium sativum tincture**
Depression due to arterial circulatory disorders.
3 times a day, add 15 drops in a small glass of water and
drink in small sips.

**Ambra 6x**
Depression with circulatory problems, nervous exhaustion
and hypersensitivity.
Vegetative disturbances
Dysregulation of the autonomic nervous system.
Can not unwind in the evening.
Vascular calcification
The person don`t like many people around, gets easily
upset.
The "Amber" type:
The person is slim, unstable, restless, lean and weak.
Blushes easily
3 times a day, take 5 globules, let them melt in your mouth.

**Ammi visnaga tincture**

Depression due to a weak heart.

Cerebral circulatory disorders

Circulatory disorders of the heart.

Ammi visnaga relaxes the coronary arteries. Thus, the body is better supplied with oxygen and nutrients.

Chest tightness and angina pectoris.

Stimulates blood flow to the heart.

3 times a day, add 15 drops in a small glass of water. Drink in small sips.


**Ammonium carb 12x** (Ammonium carbonicum D12)

Depression, high blood pressure and immunodeficiency of thick women, panting and gasping for air.

For the treatment of acidification and overload with toxins.

The patient is restless, fearful, angry and short of breath.

The person promises much, but does nothing.

Watery and red eyes.

Prone Skin

Worsening of the symtoms at night.

2 times a day, take 5 globules, let them melt in your mouth.

**Angelica tincture**
Depression
Purifies and detoxifies the body.
To strengthen the digestive system and metabolism.
Strengthens blood circulation and the immune system. The majority of our immune system is located in the abdomen.
Gastritis and stomach diseases.
Calms the entire abdomen.
Diabetes
Weakness of the digestive organs.
Stimulates the blood flow to stomach, pancreas and liver and normalizes the function of the digestive organs.
Intestines healthy, people healthy!
3 times a day, add 15 drops in some water and drink in small sips.

**Anhalonium 6x**

Depression

Modalities:

Worse especially at lunchtime.

Improvement while lying down and at night.

Associated symptom: Lameness and numbness

3 times a day, take 5 globules, let them melt in your mouth.

**Apis 12x**

Depression with worsening of symptoms at night.

The typical "Apis patient" is apathetic, indifferent, joyless and jealous.

He does not tolerate heat and has no thirst.

2 times a day, take 5 globules, let them melt in your mouth.

**Apium graveolens tincture**
Depression
Obesity and edema
Extracts metabolic waste and edema out of the body.
3 times a day, add 15 drops in some water and drink in small sips.

**Apocynum cannabinum 3x**
Depression due to a weakness of the heart and kidneys.
For the treatment of acidification and overload with toxins.
Stimulates the heart and kidneys.
Stimulates the elimination of edema.
3 times a day, take 10 globules, let them melt in your mouth.

**Aranea diadema 6x**

Depression

Modalities:

Worse by cold and damp weather.

Better by motion in fresh air.

3 times a day, take 5 globules, let them melt in your mouth.

**Argentum nitricum 6x**

Depression

Good for consumptive people who are prone to swollen glands, rashes and chronic diseases.

The face is dark and has a dried-up appearance.

The person is always in a hurry, hectic and restless.

He believes the time passes by too slowly.

He like to have salty food and cool fresh air.

Demands also for sweets and sugar, but he can not tolerate.

The patient suffers from anxiety, haste and bloating.

Argentum nitricum strengthens the immune system of consumptive people.

The person catch quickly a cold.

3 times a day, take 5 globules, let them melt in your mouth.

**Arnica tincture**
Depression due to diseases of the blood vessels.
Dizziness during head movements.
Promotes blood circulation and strengthens the blood vessels.
Diseases of the arteries and veins.
Arnica is the main remedy for arterial and venous circulatory disorders. As a result, the body is better supplied with oxygen and nutrients and the metabolism will be strengthened.
3 times a day, add 15 drops in a small glass of water and drink in small sips.

**Arsenicum album 12x**

Depression

Great restlessness, anxiety, fatigue.

Want always to move.

Loathing of food.

The person is sensitive to cold, choosy and frightened.

A broken and emaciated person with a weak immune system.

Cold, dull and blemished skin, sunken face with hollow eyes.

Eczema, boils, lichen, carbuncles, gangrene, shallow ulcers.

The skin is waxy, dry and flaky.

The secretions are corrosive, excoriating, watery and burning.

Polyuria (frequent urination with a lot of urine).

Great thirst

Melancholy, despair, indifference and depression.

The man is exhausted, pale, emaciated, frightened and tired of life.

Suicidal thoughts without fear.

The abdomen is sensitive to pressure.

Circulatory problems

Modalities:

Worse in cold air, outdoor, at midnight.

Improvement by heat.

2 times a day, take 5 globules, let them melt in your mouth.

**Asarum europaeum 6x**

Depression and nervous weakness.

Hypersensitivity of the sensory organs.

The person is extremely sensitive to noise.

Compressive pain in the head.

3 times a day, take 5 globules, let them melt in your mouth.

**Aurum iodatum 6x** (Aurum jodatum D6)

Depression

A corpulent person with high blood pressure and red face.

Sclerosis of the brain.

The person will be increasingly depressed, irritable and jaded.

Decline in memory. A grumpy patient.

The main symptoms:

Worries about the future, even if he's okay.

Always takes everything very seriously.

The accompanying symptom: Great sensitivity to cold.

3 times a day, take 5 globules, let them melt in your mouth.

**Aurum metallicum 6x**

Depression of the red-cheeked and obese people.

Sclerosis of the brain.

The person will be increasingly depressed, irritable and jaded.

Decline in memory.

Immunodeficiency, cardiac insufficiency and angina pectoris.

Circulatory problems and high blood pressure (hypertension) with red face.

Arteriosclerosis and atherosclerosis caused by metabolic blockade.

Suppuration and inflammation of the intestinal mucosa.

Aurum metallicum strengthens the immune system and eliminates metabolic blockages.

Induration of glandular organs.

A grumpy patient.

Hopeless blackness. He talks about death.

Aurum metallicum supports weight loss and increases well-being.

The main symptoms:

Worries about the future, even if he's okay.

Always takes everything very seriously.

The accompanying symptom: Great sensitivity to cold.

3 times a day, take 5 globules, let them melt in the mouth.

**Baryta carbonica 12x** (Barium carbonicum D12)
Depression of the elderly.
Fast, full and hard pulse.
Barium carbonicum relaxes the arteries and is one of the
most important remedies for age.
Stimulates the brain metabolism.
Shyness
People are slow in thinking.
Exacerbation of their symptoms by cold.
Improvement by many pats and physical attention.
An important lymphatic remedy to treat depression.
2 times a day, take 5 globules, let them melt in your mouth.

**Barium iodatum 6x** (Barium jodatum D3)
Depression due to arteriosclerosis.
Stimulates the brain metabolism.
Strengthens the immune system.
Immunodeficiency due to an underactive thyroid (slows the
metabolism).
Barium iodatum strengthens the thyroid. This stimulates the
metabolism.
Stimulates the arterial blood flow too. Thus, the bodies
cells are better supplied with oxygen and nutrients.
3 times a day, take 5 globules, let them melt in your mouth.

## Belladonna 30x

Depression

Anxiety, restlessness, nervousness.

A feeling as the head would burst.

Improvement in darkness and silence.

Rush of blood to the head.

Sudden onset of the symptoms and sudden termination.

Modalities:

Hypersensitivity of the senses to light, noise, vibration and odors.

Worse from noise, light, touch, vibration, wind and cold.

Improvement in a warm room, with heat in general and at rest.

Associated symptom: Cramps and twitching of the muscles.

In the morning take 5 globules, let them melt in your mouth.

**Berberis 3x**

Depression

To deacidify and detoxify the body.

Supports the function of the liver and pancreas.

Diseases of the liver and gallbladder.

Diabetes

3 times a day, take 10 globules, let it melt in the mouth.

**Bismutum subnitricum 6x**

Depression

The loneliness is unbearable.

Restlessness, anxiety.

Improvement of the symptoms by constantly walking around.

Associated symptoms:

Nausea and vomiting.

Paralysis and twitching of the muscles.

3 times a day, take 5 globules, let them melt in the mouth.

**Cactus 3x**

Depression due to cardiac insufficiency.

Cerebral circulatory disorders

Chest tightness

Cactus stimulates blood flow to the coronary arteries.

Feeling hot

High blood pressure

3 times a day, take 10 globules, let them melt in the mouth.

**Calcarea 12x** (Calcium carbonicum D12)

Depression

Neurasthenia, nervous weakness

For deacidification and detoxification.

Old and obstinate constipation, persistent bloating.

Regurgitation and vomiting.

The patient is gloomy, moody and indifferent.

An important remedy of "lymphatic constitution" for the treatment of metabolic syndrome, depression, weakness, immune deficiency and slow metabolism.

Rashes and frequent colds.

Sour sweat after the slightest exertion on the head and neck.

Strong foot perspiration

A fearful and hesitant person.

Aggravation of symptoms by cold and damp weather, during full moon.

Improvement by heat and drought.

2 times a day, take 5 globules, let them melt in your mouth.

## Calendula tincture
Depression
To deacidify and detoxify the body.
Purifies the body and blood.
Strengthens the lymphatic system (important for the
treatment of depression).
Increases the metabolic function.
Invigorating the blood vessels and lymph vessels.
An excellent wound healing remedy.
Eliminates inflammations
3 times a day, add 15 drops in some water and drink in
small sips.

## Capsicum 6x
Depression
Has a warming effect and stimulates the metabolism.
Capsicum dissolves fat deposits.
General chilliness
Burning of the skin and mucous membranes.
For the treatment of mucous membranes and
gastrointestinal tract.
3 times a day, take 5 globules, let them melt in your mouth.

**Carbo vegetabilis 12x**

Depression´s in old age.

Strengthens the defense force of the elderly. The remedy of age (besides Barium carb).

Great weakness, exhaustion, fatigue, lack of air and faint inclination.

Poor general condition, especially in old age.

Strong desire for fresh air and cool despite chilliness.

The modalities:

Worsening of symptoms at night and from warmth.

Improvement by fresh air.

2 times a day, take 5 globules, let them melt in your mouth.

**Carduus marianus tincture**

Depression

Metabolic disorders, acidification of the body, overload with toxins and obesitiy due to liver and gall bladder diseases.

Supports the metabolism of pancreas and liver. This is important to treat depression.

3 times a day, add 15 drops in some water and drink in small sips.

## Causticum 6x

Depression

The thinking is unclear and inhibited, mentally like paralyzed.

Fear of misfortune and death.

Sleeplessness

Nervous person, easily startled.

Hypersensitive to touch and noises.

Keynote: Pain mostly on the right side of the body.

Modalities:

Worse in dry cold weather and cold air.

Improvement at the onset of rainy weather and moisture.

Associated symptoms:

Spasms, paralysis and crippling weakness.

The patient is chilly and thirstless.

3 times a day, take 5 globules, let them melt in your mouth.

## Ceanothus 4x

If depression is related to the spleen, for example after splenectomy or disease of the spleen.

Depression after gonorrhea.

The patient can not lay on his left side.

Dirty and yellowish coated tongue.

Anemia

3 times a day, take 10 globules, let them melt in your mouth.

## China 4x

Depression

Acidification of the body and overload with toxins.

China strengthens the metabolism, immune system, pancreas and liver.

Bitter taste, yellowish coated tongue.

Abdominal pressure, bloating, diarrhea, nausea and vomiting.

Frequent common colds and attacks of fever.

Modalities:

Periodic pain at certain times of day.

Improvement by firm pressure and fresh air.

Accompanying symptom: Painful hair

Circulatory problems, meteorosensitivity and neurasthenia.

Anemia

Insomnia due to flood of thoughts. General fatigue and exhaustion.

Physical and emotional hypersensitivity.

General weakness and debility.

He does not tolerate fruit or milk.

Worsening of symptoms with a light touch, drafts, cold and after the loss of body fluids.

The person is never really healthy. Subfebrile body temperature (mild fever, often after antibiotic treatment).

3 times a day, take 10 globules, let them melt in your mouth.

## Chininum sulfuricum 4x

Depression

An important remedy for recurrent health problems.

Anemia, dizziness and physical weakness.

3 times a day, take 5 globules. Let them melt in your mouth.

## Cichorium tincture

Depression

Acidification of the body and overload with toxins due to a weakness of pancreas and liver.

Strengthens liver and pancreas.

Promotes bile formation to reduce cholesterol levels.

Diabetes

3 times a day, add 15 drops in some water and drink in small sips.

## Cimicifuga 12x

Depression of women due to hormonal imbalances and in menopause.

Cimicifuga regulates the female hormonal balance.

Nervous agitation of women in menopause.

The women is depressed and anxious.

Pain in the abdomen and chest.

Defense weakness of women by hormonal imbalances during menopause.

Spurious heart pain (the heart is healthy despite complaints).

Hot flashes, nervous agitation.

Depression and insomnia.

Restlessness, fear, hysteria and delusions.

A mistrustful person.

2 times a day, take 5 globules, let them melt in your mouth.

## Cocculus 6x

Depression

Dizziness

Trembling of the limbs.

Meteorosensitivity with excitement and nervousness.

Calcification of the cerebral vessels.

Nervous twitching of the eyes.

He feels weak and exhausted.

Keynotes:

The person is slow on the uptake, hasty nature especially in speaking.

Apprehensive over the health of other people.

The symptoms are worse in fright, grief, worry, anger and in fresh air.

Associated symptoms:

Feeling of emptiness and hollowness in the head.

Numbness, dizziness with nausea during head lifting and generally in movement.

3 times a day, take 5 globules, let them melt in your mouth.

**Colocynth 6x** (Clocynthis D6)

Depression

Modalities:

Worse by anger, disgust and fear.

Improvement by rest.

The accompanying symptoms:

Numbness, restlessness, swelling, shivering

3 times a day, take 5 globules. Let them melt in your mouth.

**Conium 6x**

Depression with dizziness and tinnitus.

Ringing in the ears.

Aggravation by turning the head sideways and turning over in bed.

Circulatory problems due to poor circulation.

Calcification of the cerebral blood vessels.

Mood swings

Indigestion

3 times a day, take 5 globules, let them melt in your mouth.

## Convallaria tincture

Depression due to heart failure.

Convallaria strengthens the heart.

Low blood pressure

Cardiac insufficiency and arrhythmias

3 times a day, add 15 drops in a small glass of water. Drink in small sips.

## Crataegus tincture

Depression due to cardiac insufficiency (lead to hypoxia of the brain cells).

Crataegus invigorates circulation of the heart.

Prevents calcification of the coronary vessels.

Circulatory problems and nervous heart.

Disturbance of blood pressure.

Arrhythmias and angina pectoris.

A perfect remedy for heart care.

3 times a day, add 15 drops in a small glass of water and drink in small sips.

**Crocus 6x**
Depression
Concentration problems
Mood swings
To improve the blood flow to the brain.
3 times a day, take 5 globules, let them melt in your mouth.

**Cynara scolymus tincture** (artichoke)
Depression
Metabolic syndrome, acidification of the body and overload
with toxins due to an insufficient pancreas- and liver
function.
Stimulates the pancreas, liver and gall bladder system. This
is very important in the treatment of depression.
Strengthens the liver and assists in detoxification.
An excellent protection for liver and pancreas.
3 times a day, add 15 drops in a small glass of water and
drink in small sips.

**Equisetum tincture**
Depression
An excellent remedy for deacidification and detoxification
of the body.
Purifies and detoxifies the body.
Also an excellent remedy for the extraction of edema.
Equisetum purifies the urinary tract.
Strengthens the kidneys, blood vessels and connective
tissue.
Contains silica (important to treat depression)
3 times a day, add 15 drops in a small glass of water and
drink in small sips.

**Ferrum metallicum 12x**
Depression and nervous weakness.
Utter discouragement
Suicidal ideation
2 times a day, take 5 globules, let them melt in your mouth.

**Fucus vesiculosus 6x**

Depression due to a weak thyroid.

Stimulates the thyroid gland, metabolism and digestion.

Do not take if an overactive thyroid.

3 times a day, take 5 globules, let them melt in your mouth.

**Fumaria tincture**

Depression due to a weak metabolism.

Stimulates the whole metabolism of the body.

Weak liver

3 times a day, add 15 drops in a small glass of water and drink in small sips.

**Galium 6x**

Depression

A very important remedy in all chronic diseases.

Strengthens the immune system.

Prevents the degeneration of brain cells.

3 times a day, take 5 globules, let them melt in your mouth.

**Gelsemium 12x**

Depression associated with a "band feeling" around the head.

Palpitations and arrhythmias.

Nervous heart disorders and headache.

Associated symptoms:

Tremor

Great exhaustion.

Modalities:

Aggravation from humid air, thunderstorms and heat.

Worse by emotional arousal, such as fright, anxiety, bad news, by thinking of the discomfort, exercise, tobacco, at 10 clock in the morning and excitement.

Improvement due to the disposal plenty bright urine, alcohol and fresh air.

Nervepain, paralysis and cramps.

2 times a day, take 5 globules, let them melt in your mouth.

**Gentiana tincture**

Depression

Arteriosclerosis and atherosclerosis

Anemia and iron deficiency.

Strengthens the digestive organs.

Promotes the formation of blood.

Contains iron

Strengthens the spleen (important for the treatment of depression).

Promotes iron absorption in the small intestine.

3 times a day, add 15 drops in a small glass of water. Drink in small sips.

**Germanium 6x**

Depression

Germanium plays an important role in the immune system.
Germanium extracts toxins out of the body. Even
environmental toxins (causing blockades in the
metabolism) such as heavy metals, mercury from amalgam
dental fillings and cadmium can be neutralized by
germanium.

In sick people with depression often the flow of body
energy is weakened or blocked. Germanium can dissolve
blockages, bring the energy back into balance and so start a
healing process.

3 times a day, take 5 globules, let them melt in your mouth.

**Ginkgo biloba tincture**

Depression due to arterial circulatory disorders.

Stimulates blood circulation of the body and improves the
oxygen uptake of the cells.

Supports arterial blood flow, thereby the defense increases.

Promotes the head blood circulation and oxygen uptake of
the blood.

Contains germanium (see above).

3 times a day, add 15 drops in a small glass of water and
drink in small sips.

**Graphites 6x**

Depression

A proven remedy for to treat chronic diseases, metabolic disorders and immune deficiency.

Helps people who are more passive and their metabolism works slowly.

Tendency to colds and skin problems.

The skin is itchy, mostly dry, scabby, yellow and pale.

Blackheads, acne

Smelling foot sweat and stinking night sweats.

Intestinal disorders

3 times a day, take 5 globules, let them melt in your mouth.

**Grindelia 6x**

Depression

Strengthens the spleen. This is very important in the treatment of depression from the naturopathic perspective.

Such as the lymph nodes, the spleen is also an important organ for strengthening the immune system.

Worsening of symptoms at night.

Feeling of suffocation.

Gasping for air.

Sleeplessness

3 times a day, take 5 globules, let them melt in your mouth.

**Hamamelis tincture**
Depression
Arteriosclerosis and atherosclerosis
Strengthens and tones the blood vessels.
3 times a day, add 15 drops in a small glass of water. Drink in small sips.

**Helleborus 3x**
Depression, acidification of the body and overload with toxins due to weak kidneys and a weak heart.
Stimulates the kidneys to extract metabolic waste and acid.
Strengthens the heart muscle.
3 times a day, take 10 globules, let them melt in the mouth.

**Helonias dioica 3x**
Depression of women
Weak connective tissue
Helonias strengthens the connective tissue of the blood vessels.
Uterine prolapse
3 times a day, take 10 globules, let them melt in your mouth.

## Hyoscyamus 6x

Depression

The person grumbles and rages.

Violent excitement, which then turns into a depression.

Insomnia and restlessness

The person is irritable and sensitive.

When necessary, every 20 minutes take 5 globules. Let them melt in your mouth.

## Hypericum tincture

Depression

Nervousness

A classic remedy for mental illness.

Irritability.

Affects mood enhancing, tonic and vegetative balancing.

3 times a day, add 15 drops in a small glass of water and drink in small sips.

**Ignatia 6x**

Depression with nervous disorders, insomnia and mood swings.

Exacerbation of symptoms due to mental excitement and distress.

Headache

Ever-changing moods.

Hunger despite aversion to food.

Insomnia during menopause.

3 times a day, take 5 globules, let them melt in your mouth.

**Iodine 6x** (Jodum D6)

Depression due to an underactive thyroid gland.

Diabetes

An important remedy for thyroid and pancreas.

The metabolism is stimulated and the immune system strengthened.

Bloating, constipation and emaciation.

Arteriosclerosis (leading to an insufficient supply of oxygen and nutrients to body cells).

Hypothyroidism

3 times a day, take 5 globules, let them melt in your mouth.

**Kali carb 12x** (Kalium carbonicum D12)

Depression

To strengthen the immune system from people with physical, intellectual and emotional weakness.

The thyroid is underactive (causes depression and immunodeficiency).

Bad breath, like cheese.

Weakness in the abdomen. After eating the symptoms are more worse.

General physical, mental and spiritual weakness.

Constant fear, fear of the future, of death. What should I do if .....

Tendency to cold.

Stinging and wandering pain.

Bags on the upper eyelids.

Sweating by the slightest exertion.

Fear of being alone. A frightful person.

Hypersensitivity to pain and noise.

Bad memory and daytime sleepiness.

2 times a day, take 5 globules, let them melt in your mouth.

**Kalium jodatum 6x** (Potassium iodatum D6)
Depression due to arteriosclerosis.
The patient seeks to relieve his discomfort in fresh air and wind.
Sharp, watery, thin, cool, green secretions of the skin.
Aggravation of symptoms in warm clothes and warm room.
Improvement in movement.
Regulates blood vessel tension.
Arterial circulatory disorders.
Strengthens the immune system.
Stimulates the thyroid gland.
Promotes blood circulation to the brain.
3 times a day, take 5 globules, let them melt in your mouth.

**Kreosotum 6x**
Depression due to diabetes.
Arterial circulatory disorders caused by diabetes.
Pulsation of the blood vessels.
Dizziness, neurasthenia and vomiting.
Vision problems and weakness of memory.
The modalities:
Worsening of symptoms in fresh air, by cold food, cold drinks and cold weather.
Improvement by heat, hot drinks and exercise.
The accompanying symptoms:
Emaciated
The skin is pale or yellowish.
Chilliness, rapid emaciation and weakness.
Irritability and bad mood.
3 times a day, take 5 globules, let them melt in your mouth.

**Lachesis 12x**

Depression of women in menopause.

Circulatory problems and dizziness when waking up.

Very pale face.

Feeling as drunkenness.

Mood swings

Nervousness and menopausal symptoms.

Anxiety in enclosed and confined rooms, sometimes even in large spaces.

Startle during sleep and exhaustion after sleep.

Can not bear tight clothing, especially around the neck.

Infectious diseases, inflammation of the skin and mucous membranes.

3 times a day, take 5 globules, let them melt in your mouth.

**Leonurus cardiaca tincture**

Depression with low blood pressure and rapid pulse.

Heart problems and circulatory disorders.

Normalizes heart function

3 times a day, add 15 drops in a small glass of water. Drink in small sips.

**Leptandra 3x**

Depression due to diabetes.

Regenerates the function of pancreatic tissue.

Inflammation of the liver and gall bladder system.

3 times a day, take 10 globules, let them melt in your mouth.

**Levisticum tincture**
Depression
Metabolic disorders, acidification of the body, overload
with toxins and edema due to cardiac and renal weakness.
To deacidify and detoxify the body.
Promotes blood circulation of the urogenital tract.
3 times a day, add 15 drops in a small glass of water and
drink in small sips.

**Lithium carb 4x** (Lithium carbonicum D4)
Depression
To deacidify and detoxify the body.
Purifies the body.
Gout and rheumatic diseases.
High uric-acid-level in the blood.
3 times a day, take 10 globules, let them melt in your
mouth.

## Lycopodium 6x

Depression

Stimulates digestion and metabolism of the body to extract acids, toxins and metablic waste.

Stops the nightly cravings and cravings for sweets.

Aggravation of symptoms between 4 clock in the afternoon (4 pm) and 8 clock in the evening (8 pm), through heat, touch, anger and tight clothing.

Feeling of helplessness.

Complaints mostly on the right side of the body.

The typical "Lycopodium type" requires sweets, sugar and hot drinks.

He is nasty on awakening, but otherwise the symptoms are better in the morning.

Flatulence and bloating even after eating small amounts.

Irascibility, brooks no contradiction.

Disorders of pancreas and liver function.

Inflammation and disorders of the hepatobiliary system.

Swelling of the liver, obstinate constipation.

Sour vomiting

Flatulence and rumbling in the abdomen.

Much gas formation in the stomach, a loud rumbling and gurgling in the bowels.

Heartburn and great fatigue after eating.

Constant burping

Saturated after little food.

Improvement by belching, by hot food and drinks, exercise and cold air.

The pain is chronic and burning.

Kidney stones

The "Lycopodium patient" has two strange symptoms:

"He weeps, if somebody would like to thank him" and "one foot is warm, the other foot is cold".

3 times a day, take 5 globules, let them melt in your mouth.

## Melilotus tincture
Depression
Strengthens the immune system and supports the metabolism.
Extracts metabolic waste and toxins.
Weakness of the veins and lymphatic vessels. Strengthens veins and lymphatic vessels.
Improves blood and lymph flow.
Thins the blood.
Strengthens the connective tissue.
Venous circulation disorders.
3 times a day, add 15 drops in a small glass of water and drink in small sips.

## Mercurius corossivus 6x
Depression caused by degenerative blood vessels.
Weakness of memory
3 times a day, take 5 globules, let them melt in your mouth.

## Millefolium tincture
Depression
To deacidify and detoxify the body.
Relaxes and calms the entire abdomen.
Promotes the circulation of the digestive organs.
Bloating
Strengthens the spleen (important for the treatment of depression)
Promotes iron absorption in the small intestine.
Promotes blood circulation and strengthens the blood vessels. As a result, the body is better supplied with oxygen and nutrients and the metabolism will be strengthened.
Strengthens the immune system.
3 times a day, add 15 drops in a small glass of water and drink in small sips.

**Natrum muriaticum 12x**

The person is melancholic and depressed.

Jealousy as a result of loss of love.

The skin has blackheads and sores.

Natrum muriaticum promotes blood circulation.

The person has in generell a poor blood circulation.

Digestive problems and kidney problems.

Tendency to colds.

Nausea, vomiting

Will not be comforted, being resentful, tearful and sensitive.

The patient feels ill in the morning, like to eat salty and spicy.

Clumsy, throwing things down from nervousness.

Worse by employment.

Weakening, losing weight even with good nutrition.

Crying without reason, but consolation bother.

Can not pass urine when other people around.

Morning headaches

Chronic constipation, but also chronic enteritis (diarrhea).

Natrum muriaticum purifies the body fluids.

2 times a day, take 5 globules, let them melt in your mouth.

**Nux moschata 6x**

Depression

He is indifferent, apathetic and sleepy.

Has a dry mouth without thirst.

Worsening of symptoms by cold.

3 times a day, take 5 globules, let them melt in your mouth.

## Nux vomica 6x

Depression due to stress and anger with a feeling of constriction.

Consequences of alcohol abuse.

Feeling as if a nail in the head.

Modalities:

Worse after midnight, early morning, by cold and dry weather, after drinking wine and coffee.

Improvement in wet weather, in warm room.

Overwrought nerves (manager types), nausea and vomiting of drunkards.

Tendency to convulsions and periodic complaints.

Circulatory problems with vertigo, especially after stimulant abuse (alcohol, nicotine).

A feeling of constriction.

The "Nux Vomica Type": Irritable, choleric, nervous, lively, emaciated.

Disease of the pancreas due to alcohol abuse.

Swelling of the liver

Gallstones

Inflammation of the bile ducts.

Fever

Hourly take 5 globules, let them melt in your mouth.

**Okoubaka**

Depression

Toxins (for example food additives) block the metabolism.
This causes acidification and overload with toxins.
Okoubaka detoxifies the body, dissolves metabolic
blockages, eliminates and extracts metabolic waste and
environmental toxins.
Strengthens the immune system. Helps therefore good for
the treatment of depression.

For thorough detoxification, elimination and extraction of
environmental toxins and other residues, please make the
following treatment. In addition, please drink the above
mentioned teas.

1st to 4th week:
Okoubaka D3
3 times a day, take 10 globules, let them melt in your
mouth.

5th to 8th week:
Okoubaka D4
3 times a day, take 10 globules, let them melt in your
mouth.

9th to 12th week:
Okoubaka D6
3 times a day, take 5 globules, let them melt in your mouth.

13th to 16th week: Okoubaka D12
2 times a day, take 5 globules, let them melt in your mouth.

Then a further 3 months: Okoubaka D30
1 time a week, take 5 globules, let them melt in your
mouth.

## Phosphorus amorphus 12x

Depression

The person hear the echo of his own voice.

Feeling as if clogged ears.

An important metabolic remedy.

Strengthens the function of the liver, pancreas and immune system.

A slender and frosty man.

Afraid of darkness, loneliness and thunderstorms.

Self-pity

Labile moods, he likes to be comforted.

Phosphorus is known in naturopathy as a light bringer.

The "Phosphorus type" likes salt, cold drinks and ice cream.

He is afraid of darkness, aloneness and thunderstorms, is tall and slim, has fine hair.

Aroused quickly

Reacts violently to everything.

The man is exhausted quickly.

Night sweats

Keynotes:

Scary, especially at dusk.

He is slim, tall, blonde.

Bleed easily

2 times a day, take 5 globules, let them melt in your mouth.

## Platinum 12x

Depression

An arrogant person

2 times a day, take 5 globules, let them melt in your mouth.

## Plumbum aceticum 30x

Depression with the feeling of pins and needles.

Nervousness and pale face.

Paralysis of the intestinal motility (constipation).

Mouth and gum ulcers.

In the morning take 5 globules, let them melt in your mouth.

## Psorinum 12x

Depression

For the treatment of persistent metabolic disorders (cause depression).

The typical "Psorinum patient" is frosty, cautious, afraid to wash and has an unpleasant perspiration.

Desperate anxiety

Chronic eczema and dermatitis.

Obstinate and itchy skin conditions

The skin is usually dry, pale and yellow.

Stinking foot sweat and stinking night sweats.

Lichen, scabs, acne and blackheads.

Aggravation of symptoms from cold, sun, wind, and when changing from warm to cold weather.

Improvement by rest, when lying down and through eating.

2 times a day, take 5 globules, let them melt in your mouth.

**Pulsatilla 12x**

Depression

The "Pulsatilla Type" is moody, sensitive and whiny, loves compassion.

Chilliness, lack of appetite and without thirst.

Worsening of symptoms at night.

Improvement by exercise in the fresh air.

Neurasthenia

Hypersensitive to noise.

Self-pity

Moody, wants comfort, gentle, melancholy and anxious.

Has fear of death.

Dizziness

The person is afraid of people.

Keynote: Soft and gentle disposition, shy, timid, tearful, chilly, anemic.

2 times a day, take 5 globules, let them melt in your mouth.

**Rhizoma helenii tincture**

An excellent metabolic remedy for the treatment of depression.

To deacidify and detoxify the body.

Stimulates digestion and metabolism of the body to extract acids, toxins and metablic waste.

Strengthens and regenerates pancreas and liver.

Strengthens the immune system.

Diabetes

3 times a day, add 15 drops in a small glass of water and drink in small sips.

**Rhododendron 6x**

Depression

Bad weather and the approach of a storm or lightning storm can be predicted by pain, depression and nervousness. Immediately after a storm he is relaxed and feels good.

Modalities:

Worse before and during storms, by wind cold and damp, by cold, touch, pressure and rest.

Improvement through food, heat, after a storm and the rising of the barometer.

3 times a day, take 5 globules, let them melt in your mouth.

**Rosmarinus tincture**

Depression

Stimulates the metabolism, blood circulation and the immune system.

Arterial circulatory disturbances

Low blood pressure

Strengthens the heart and blood vessels.

Purifies and detoxifies the heart muscle.

Very good for the treatment of rheumatism and metabolic acidosis.

Detoxifies the muscles

3 times a day, add 15 drops in a small glass of water and drink in small sips.

**Ruta graveolens 3x**
Depression due to arteriosclerosis and atherosclerosis.
Ruta strengthens and purifies the connective tissue of the blood vessels.
Stimulates blood circulation.
3 times a day, take 10 globules, let them melt in your mouth.

**Sanguinaria 6x**
Depression of women in menopause.
Loss of smell and taste.
Hypersensitive to cold and weather changes, wind and "every change of clothes".
The symptoms appear and disappear with the sun.
Dizziness and symptoms of menopause.
Meteorosensitivity with headache.
Burning of the hands and feet.
Always red face.
3 times a day, take 5 globules, let them melt in your mouth.

**Secale cornutum 6x**
Depression due to atherosclerosis.
Improves blood circulation.
Arterial circulatory disturbances.
Improvement of symptoms by cold applications.
Aggravation from heat and movement.
3 times a day, take 5 globules, let them melt in your mouth.

**Sepia 12x**

Depression and anxiety

The patient sighs, moans and smiles alternately.

Anxious and irritable.

The "sepia type" has a yellowish complexion, hates compassion and wants to be left alone.

Mentally sluggish

Rapid change of mood

Indifferent to obligations

The stomach feels empty and desolate. The hepatic region is painful and stinging.

Brown spots on the skin of the abdomen.

Diarrhea after milk consumption.

2 times a day, take 5 globules, let them melt in your mouth.

**Solidago tincture**

Depression

Extracts water retentions

To deacidify and detoxify the body.

To stimulate the blood cleansing and extraction via the kidneys.

Diuretic

To stimulate the kidneys.

3 times a day, add 15 drops in a small glass of water and drink in small sips.

**Spigelia 6x**

Depression

Increase and decrease of the symptoms with the movement of the sun.

Fear of sharp objects.

Worse are the symptoms from motion, touch, noise, vibration, storm, weather changes, cold air and by stooping.

Associated symptoms:

Heart anxiety

Shivering and chills all over the body.

3 times a day, take 5 globules, let them melt in your mouth.

**Spongia 6x**

Depression due to an underactive thyroid gland.

Stimulates the thyroid gland. So the body temperature increases. The immune system and metabolism are strengthened.

3 times a day, take 5 globules, let them melt in your mouth.

**Stannum 12x**

Depression

Weakness, especially in the chest.

Nerve and muscle weakness.

Legs and knees tremble.

Believe to have a lung disease.

Always want to cry, but crying worse.

Kitchen smell causes vomiting.

Each task is too much.

2 times a day take 5 globules, let them melt in your mouth.

## Staphysagria 12x

Depression

Staphysagria is a great remedy for suppressed anger and repressed emotions.

Great indignation about things that were done by others or himself.

Keynotes:

Sensitive to what others think about him.

Deep-set eyes with blue edges as after a night of drinking.

Modalities:

Worse at night, by anger and indignation.

Improvement of the symptoms after breakfast, by heat and bed rest.

2 times a day, take 5 globules, let them melt in your mouth.

## Sulphur 12x

An important remedy to treat depression.

Sulfur is an important catalyst to bring a stalled metabolism and immune system back on track.

Chronic diseases

Detoxifying the body

Inflammation and ulceration of the skin.

The skin looks gray, dirty and wrinkled.

Itching and burning at night.

Stabbing pains in the liver.

Long-term illnesses

Stinking flatulence in the morning.

Appetite for everything, especially on fat.

Pushes away the cover at night, stretching his legs out of bed.

Redness of the orifices.

Sharp and excoriating secretions.

Strengthens the immune system.

Regenerates the pancreas and liver.

2 times a day, take 5 globules, let them melt in your mouth.

**Symphytum tincture**

Depression due to arteriosclerosis and atherosclerosis.
Strengthens the connective tissue and the muscles of the
blood vessels.
Strengthens the connective tissue in its metabolic function.
Promotes hepatic blood flow and is important for the small
intestine.
Promotes the formation of blood.
Contains iron and vitamin B12.
3 times a day, add 15 drops in a small glass of water and
drink in small sips.

**Syzygium tincture**

Depression due to diabetes.
Metabolic disorders
Strengthens the function of pancreas, liver and gallbladder.
Proven in diabetes
3 times a day, add 15 drops in a small glass of water and
drink in small sips.

**Tarantula 6x**

Depression with insomnia and irritability ("as if stung by a
tarantula").
Hourly take 5 globules, let them melt in your mouth.

**Taraxacum tincture** (dandelion)
Depression due to weakness and diseases of the liver, kidneys and bile.
Strengthens the liver-bile system, the pancreas and kidneys.
Detoxifies the liver and acts cholagogue.
Strengthens the immune system.
Cleans the blood and stimulates the metabolism.
Nausea due to a weakness of pancreas and liver.
3 times a day, add 15 drops in a small glass of water and drink in small sips.

**Urtica urens tincture**
Depression
Purifies and detoxifies the body.
Stimulates the kidneys and metabolism to extract acids, toxins and metabolic waste.
Itchy and inflamed skin rash with small pimples and blisters.
Diuretic
3 times a day, add 15 drops in a small glass of water and drink in small sips.

**Viscum album tincture**

Depression

Cerebale circulatory disorders

Has a normalizing effect in the treatment of low- and high blood pressure.

Dizziness caused by cerebral (in the brain) circulation disorders.

3 times a day, add 15 drops in a small glass of water and drink in small sips.

**Zinkum valerianicum 12x**

Depression with nervousness.

The person is restless and has a restlessness in the legs (restless legs).

Poor sleep

Twitching in bed, like electric shocks.

2 times a day, take 5 globules, let them melt in your mouth.

Homeopathic recipes to treat depression due to circulatory disorders.

1) Homeopathic prescription to treat depression due to arteriosclerosis:
Arnica 3x, Potassium iodatum 6x (Kalium jodatum D6) aa 25.0
3 times a day, add 15 drops in a small glass of water and drink in small sips.

2) In general circulatory disorders:
Arnica tincture, Secale cornutum 6x aa 10.0, Tincture of Gingko biloba ad 50.0
3 times a day, add 15 drops in a small glass of water and drink in small sips.

3) Sanicula tincture, Millefolium tincture aa 50.0
3 times a day, add 15 drops in a small glass of water and drink in small sips.

4) Depression due to arteriosclerosis and circulatory problems of women in menopause:
Secale cornutum 6x 10.0, Potassium iodatum 6x (Kalium jodatum D6) 10.0, Cimicifuga 6x 10.0
3 times a day, add 15 drops in a small glass of water and drink in small sips.

5) Depression due to circulatory disorders of the coronary arteries:
Potassium iodatum 4x (potassium is very important for the function of the heart muscle), Arnica tincture (vasodilator), Cactus grandiflorus 3x aa 10.0, Extractum Crataegi 20.0
3 times a day, add 15 drops in a small glass of water and drink in small sips.

Homoepathic recipe to stimulate the metabolism (important for the treatment of depression):
Helianthus tuberosus 3x dil., Duboisia 3x dil., Euphorbia cyparissias 3x dil. aa 10.0, Extractum Fucus vesiculosus (if not overactive thyroid occurs), Extr Frangulae (buckthorn bark) and extract of Alchemilla (lady's mantle) aa 15.0
3 times a day, add 15 drops in a small glass of water and drink in small sips.

A recipe for strengthening the pancreas, liver and bile (important in the treatment of depression):
Cardui marianae tincture, Cardui benedikti tincture aa 25.0, China tincture, Chelidonium 6x aa 10.0, Flor de Piedra 6x 30.0
3 times a day, add 15 drops in a small glass of water and drink in small sips.

Also homeopathic remedies for the lymphatic system are important to treat depression. These remedies stimulate the extraction of acids, metabolic waste and toxins. They also purify and strengthen the function of the connective tissue and stimulate the immune system.

Therefore you also should take one of the following remedies:

1) Badiaga 12x
For 4 weeks, 2 times a day, take 5 globules. Let them melt in your mouth.

2) Baryta carbonica 12x (Barium carbonicum D12)
For 4 weeks, 2 times a day, take 5 globules. Let them melt in your mouth.

3) Barium iodatum 12x (Barium jodatum D12)
For 4 weeks, 2 times a day, take 5 globules. Let them melt in your mouth.

4) Calcarea 12x (Calcium carbonicum D12)
For 4 weeks, 2 times a day, take 5 globules. Let them melt in your mouth.

5) Mercury solubilis 12x (Mercurius solubilis D12)
For 4 weeks, 2 times a day, take 5 globules. Let them melt in your mouth.

6) Thuja 12x
For 4 weeks, 2 times a day, take 5 globules. Let them melt in your mouth.

## Depression - Treatment with Schuessler salts

Prerequisite to avoid and to treat depression is a balanced acid-base-balance, proper nutrition and good blood circulation. Nutrition is a key factor in the treatment of our metabolism and health.

With a balanced and varied diet the body will be supplied with all the necessary nutrients. The cells and organs are strengthened.

At the same time you support your immune system, your metabolism and ensure a perfect acid-base-balance, the foundation of our health. Proper nutrition also helps to extract toxins from the body and dissolves healing blockages.

Remember: There are several metabolic blockages which you have to treat for to deacidify and detoxify the body of people suffering from depression.

Metabolic blockage No. 1: The acid-base balance

Too much sugar, white flour, meat and sausage acidifies the body. In order to neutralize the acids precious bases are consumed. What is not neutralized, ends up as a "hazardous waste" in the connective tissue and leads to its acidity.

The metabolic process slows down. We get depression, gain weight despite calorie conscious diet and exercise.

Schuessler-salt No. 9 Sodium phosphate 6x (Nr. 9 Natrium phosphoricum D6) ensures that toxins and metabolic residues are flushed from the body. Sodium phosphate (Natrium phosphoricum) also stimulates the metabolism of fat and sugar degradation.

Metabolic blockage No. 2: The connective tissue

The connective tissue is more than just a connection between the organs. It serves as a nutrient storage and intermediate storage of metabolic products.

In the connective tissue the cells dispose their waste products. That the toxins can leave the body, enough mineral salts must be present.

A mineral deficiency causes metabolic residues, acidification and overload with toxins. They remain in the connective tissue and bind water. It comes to depressive moods and water retention (edema) in the tissues of the body.

The salts No. 6 Potassium sulph 6x (Nr. 6 Kalium sulfuricum D6), No. 9 Sodium phosphate 6x (Nr. 9 Natrium phosphoricum D6), No. 10 Sodium sulphate 6x (Nr. 10 Natrium sulfuricum D6) and No. 11 Silicea 12x promote the excretion of acids and toxins through the skin and activate the detoxification via the liver, intestines and kidneys.

Metabolic blockage No. 3: The digestion

Environmental pollution, lush diet and medication burden the liver, our central metabolic organ. Stomach, pancreas and intestines suffer with.

Many metabolic processes stalled and it comes to depressive moods, weight gain, constipation, bloating and stomach problems.

No. 4 Potassium chloratum 6x (Nr. 4 Kalium chloratum D6), No. 6 Potassium sulph 6x (Nr. 6 Kalium sulfuricum D6) and No. 10 Sodium sulphate 6x (Nr. 10 Natrium sulfuricum D6) give the liver and digestive organs new power. The metabolic processes accelerate. Toxins and acids are excreted faster.

Metabolic blockage No. 4: Our water Resources

Every day the organism produces acids and waste products that have to be filtered out by the kidneys. But part of it also ends up in the connective tissue, because for the removal mineral salts are absent. This forces depression.

No. 8 Sodium chloratum 6x (Nr. 8 Natrium chloratum D6) regulates the water balance and No. 10 Sodium sulphate 6x (Nr. 10 Natrium sulfuricum D6) drained. Together they control the water balance in the body.

Metabolic blockage No. 5: The protein digestion

Protein is essential for the production of enzymes, hormones, muscles and the connective tissue. However, in the cleavage of proteins ammonia is formed (a strong cytotoxin). The liver converts the ammonia into non-toxic urea, which is excreted in the urine.

Therefore, a high intake of protein is a strong decontamination work for the liver and our two kidneys. This stimulates depression.

Salt No. 9 Sodium phosphate 6x (Nr. 9 Natrium phosphoricum D6) helps the body in protein metabolism. Salt No. 6 Potassium sulph 6x (Nr. 6 Kalium sulfuricum D6) supports the liver in the degradation of ammonia.

Metabolic blockage No. 6: The digestion of fat

We need fats because they provide essential fatty acids. Fat is also the best energy storage in times of need. The body hoards it especially in the thighs and hips, the abdomen and buttocks.

But the adipose tissue is also a deposit for toxins. This forces depressive moods.

The Schuessler salts No. 6 Potassium sulph 6x (Nr. 6 Kalium sulfuricum D6), No. 9 Sodium phosphate 6x (Nr. 9 Natrium phosphoricum D6) and No. 10 Sodium sulphate 6x (Nr. 10 Natrium sulfuricum D6) help to lead out the contaminants.

## Metabolic blockage No. 7: The carbohydrate digestion

Carbohydrates are energy pure. But in abundance they are also responsible for weight gain and acidification of the body. What is not burned, will be converted and stored in fat.

Especially sweets and white flour products are dangerous. They let the blood sugar level rise up rapidly. This leads to a strong insulin release.

Insulin normalizes blood sugar. At the same time burning fat is broken. Insulin leads fats from the meal in the fat stores of the body. In addition, it holds back water in the body and causes rapidly new hunger.

The Schuessler salt No. 4 Potassium chloratum 6x (Nr. 4 Kalium chloratum D6) supports the combustion of sugar. Important are also the salts No. 6 Potassium sulph 6x (Nr. 6 Kalium sulphuricum D6) and No. 10 Sodium sulphate 6x (Nr 10 Natrium sulfuricum D6).

The combination of these salts Nos. 4, 6, 8, 9, 10 and 11 has proven itself well in the treatment of acidification and overload with toxins. Dissolve from each cell salt 1 tablet in a small glass of hot water (all together in the same glass). Drink in small sips half an hour before or after eating.

After 6 weeks make one week break, then repeat. If necessary, you can repeat this treatment several times.

In the manic phase (temper tantrums or exuberance):
No. 19 Cuprum arsenicosum 6x
No. 16 Lithium chloratum 6x and
No. 20 Potassium aluminum sulph 6x (Nr. 20 Kalium aluminium sulphuricum D6)
Alternate each remedy daily by taking 4 times a day 2 tablets. Let them melt in your mouth.

In the depressive stage:
No. 2 Calcium phosphate 6x
No. 5 Potassium phosphate 6x (Nr. 5 Kalium phosphoricum D6) and
No. 10 Sodium sulphate 6x (Nr. 10 Natrium sulphuricum D6)
Alternate each remedy daily by taking 4 times a day 2 tablets. Let them melt in your mouth.

In periods of increased restlessness, agitation and aggression:
No. 9 Sodium phosphate 6x (Nr. 9 Natrium phosphoricum D6) and
No. 16 Lithium chloratum 3x
Alternate each remedy hourly by taking 3 tablets. Let them melt in your mouth.

At risk of suicide (speaks about suicide):
No. 10 Sodium sulphate 3x (Nr. 10 Natrium sulphuricum D3)
No. 5 Potassium phosphate 6x (Nr. 5 Kalium phosphoricum D6) and
No. 16 Lithium chloratum 3x
Alternate each remedy half-hourly by taking 3 tablets. Let them melt in your mouth.

Mood swings, emotional upset, tendency to cry,
hypochondria (imaginary illness):
No. 5 Potassium phosphate 6x (Nr. 5 Kalium phosphoricum
D6) and
No. 8 Sodium chloratum 6x (Nr. 8 Natrium chloratum D6)
Alternate each remedy daily by taking 4 times a day 2
tablets. Let them melt in your mouth.

Depression, nervousness, tremor, sweating, rapid pulse:
No. 5 Potassium phosphate 6x (Nr. 5 Kalium phosphoricum
D6)
Potassium phosphate acts centrally soothing and
desensitizing.
The nutrient salt for body, mind, spirit and heart.
Stimulates recovery and reconstruction.
It brings the nerve and muscle metabolism back into
balance.
4 times a day, take 2 tablets, let them melt in your mouth.

**No. 6 Potassium sulph 6x** (Nr. 6 Kalium sulphuricum D6)
Room heat aggravates the symptoms.
Note for the budding homeopaths among my readers:
Potassium sulph is the mineralic Pulsatilla, but more
irritable and sensitive.
4 times a day, take 2 tablets, let them melt in your mouth.

**No. 8 Sodium chloratum 6x** (Nr. 8 Natrium chloratum
D6)
The patient will not be comforted, being resentful, tearful
and sensitive.
Improvement when alone.
The patient hates pity.
Has a rip in the center of the lower lip.
The patient feels ill in the morning.
He likes to eat salty and spicy.
4 times a day, take 2 tablets, let them melt in your mouth.

**No. 9 Sodium phosphate 6x** (Nr. 9 Natrium phosphoricum
D6)
Depression with additional acidity, rheumatism and gout.
4 times a day, take 2 tablets, let them melt in your mouth.

**No. 10 Sodium sulphate 6x** (Nr. 10 Natrium sulphuricum
D6)
Cleans the body juices.
4 times a day, take 2 tablets, let them melt in your mouth.

## No. 11 Silicea 12x

The depression is worse at new and full moon, weather changes.

The man is shivering constantly.

Fear of pointed objects, especially needles.

Brittle nails and white spots in the nails.

Lack of self-confidence.

Flabby muscles

Hourly take 2 tablets, let them melt in your mouth.

## No. 14 Potassium bromatum 6x (Nr. 14 Kalium bromatum D6)

Depression, employment neuroses, anxiety, insomnia.

The patient makes a lot of stress.

4 times a day, take 2 tablets, let them melt in your mouth.

## No. 21 Zincum chloratum 6x

Depression and a tendency to nervous disorders.

Neurasthenia

Cerebral irritations

4 times a day, take 2 tablets, let them melt in your mouth.

Depression, nervousness, weakness:

No. 5 Potassium phosphate 6x (Nr. 5 Kalium phosphoricum D6)

No. 7 Magnesium phosphate 6x (Nr. 7 Magnesium phosphoricum D6) and

No. 8 Sodium chloratum 6x (Nr. 8 Natrium chloratum D6) Alternate each remedy daily by taking 4 times a day 2 tablets. Let them melt in your mouth.

Biochemical health cure (Schuessler salts) for the treatment of depression. Duration of intake: 2 months

On Monday
No. 1 Calcium fluorite 12x (Nr. 1 Calcium fluoratum D12)
4 times a day, take 2 tablets, let them melt in your mouth.

On Tuesday
No. 2 Calcium phosphate 6x (Nr. 2 Calcium phosphoricum D6)
4 times a day, take 2 tablets, let them melt in your mouth.

On Wednesday
No. 11 Silicea 12x
4 times a day, take 2 tablets, let them melt in your mouth.

On Thursday
No. 3 Ferrum phos 12x (Nr. 3 Ferrum phosphoricum D12)
4 times a day, take 2 tablets, let them melt in your mouth.

On Friday
No. 7 Magnesium phosphate 6x (Nr. 7 Magnesium phosphoricum D6)
4 times a day, take 2 tablets, let them melt in your mouth.

On Saturday
No. 1 Calcium fluorite 12x
4 times a day, take 2 tablets, let them melt in your mouth.

On Sunday
No. 2 Calcium phosphate 6x
4 times a day, take 2 tablets, let them melt in your mouth.

A proven biochemical cure (Schuessler salts) for the treatment of depression because of atherosclerosis and circulatory disorders. Duration: 2 months

On Monday
No. 1 Calcium fluorite 12x
4 times a day, take 2 tablets, let them melt in your mouth.

On Tuesday
No. 3 Ferrum phos 6x
4 times a day, take 2 tablets, let them melt in your mouth.

On Wednesday
No. 5 Potassium phosphate 6x (Nr. 5 Kalium phosphoricum D6)
4 times a day, take 2 tablets, let them melt in your mouth.

On Thursday
No. 1 Calcium fluorite 12x
4 times a day, take 2 tablets, let them melt in your mouth.

On Friday
No. 7 Magnesium phosphate 6x
4 times a day, take 2 tablets, let them melt in your mouth.

On Saturday
No. 1 Calcium fluorite 12x
4 times a day, take 2 tablets, let them melt in your mouth.
On Sunday

On Sunday
No. 3 Ferrum phos 12x
4 times a day, take 2 tablets, let them melt in your mouth.

Biochemical health cure (Schuessler salts) for the treatment of depression with anxiety, hot flashes, mournfulness and irritability. Duration: 2 months

Monday
No. 7 Magnesium phosphate 6x
4 times a day, take 2 tablets, let them melt in your mouth.

Tuesday
No. 5 Potassium phosphate 6x (Nr. 5 Kalium ohosphoricum D6)
4 times a day, take 2 tablets, let them melt in your mouth.

Wednesday
No. 7 Magnesium phosphate 6x
4 times a day, take 2 tablets, let them melt in your mouth.

Thursday
No. 3 Ferrum phos 12x
4 times a day, take 2 tablets, let them melt in your mouth.

Friday
No. 7 Magnesium phosphate 6x
4 times a day, take 2 tablets, let them melt in your mouth.

Saturday
No. 5 Potassium phosphate 6x (Nr. 5 Kalium phosphoricum D6)
4 times a day, take 2 tablets, let them melt in your mouth.

Sunday
No. 3 Ferrum phos 12x
4 times a day, take 2 tablets, let them melt in your mouth.

Biochemical health cure (Schuessler salts) for the treatment of depression and sensitivity to changes in weather. Duration: 2 months

Monday
No. 7 Magnesium phosphate 6x (Nr. 7 Magnesium phosphoricum D6)
4 times a day, take 2 tablets, let them melt in your mouth.

Tuesday
No. 10 Sodium sulphate 6x (Nr. 10 Natrium sulfuricum D6)
4 times a day, take 2 tablets, let them melt in your mouth.

Wednesday
No. 7 Magnesium phosphate 6x
4 times a day, take 2 tablets, let them melt in your mouth.

Thursday
No. 6 Potassium sulph 6x (Nr. 6 Kalium sulfuricum D6)
4 times a day, take 2 tablets, let them melt in your mouth.

Friday
No. 7 Magnesium phosphate 6x
4 times a day, take 2 tablets, let them melt in your mouth.

Saturday
No. 10 Sodium sulphate 6x
4 times a day, take 2 tablets, let them melt in your mouth.

Sunday
No. 6 Potassium sulph 6x
4 times a day, take 2 tablets, let them melt in your mouth.

More information about Schuessler salts you will find in my book:

Schuessler Salts - Homeopathic cell salts for your health

**Epilogue**

I hope that you have discovered a lot of new and interesting things while reading this book.

I wish you much success in the treatment of depression with Homeopathy and Schuessler salts, and wish you joy in life and especially your health.

Robert Kopf

Made in the USA
Las Vegas, NV
11 March 2024

87034655R00056